# Picture History
## of the
## 20th Century

# THE 1940s

## Tim Wood and R.J. Unstead

## SEA-TO-SEA
*Mankato Collingwood London*

This edition first published in 2006 by
Sea-to-Sea Publications
1980 Lookout Drive
North Mankato
Minnesota 56003

Printed in China

Library of Congress Cataloging-in-Publication Data

Wood, Tim.
   The 1940's / by Tim Wood  & R.J. Unstead.
       p. cm. — (Picture history of the 20th century)
   Includes index.
   Originally published: London; New York : F. Watts, c1990.
   Summary: Text and pictures highlight the main events of the 1940s.
   ISBN 1-932889-72-8
   1. Nineteen forties—Pictorial works—Juvenile literature. 2. World War,
1939-1945--Pictorial works—Juvenile literature [1. Nineteen forties. 2. World War,
1939-1945.] I. Unstead, R.J.  II. Title. III. Series.

D422.W66 2005
909.82'4'0222—dc22
                                                            2004062525

9 8 7 6 5 4 3 2

Published by arrangement with the Watts Publishing Group Ltd, London

**Photographs:** Associated Press/World Wide 22(T), 23(T), 23(C), 23(B), 31(T), 34(BL),
36(BL); thanks to the Britten-Pears Library 41(BR); thanks to Columbia Pictures Inc
15(BR); Jan Croot 32(CR), 43(TR); John Frost Newspapers 33(CR), 33(B); GEC
Marconi 29(TL); Mary Evans Picture Library 8(T), 33(TL); Hulton-Deutsch 28(T),
29(BL), 29(BR), 40(BR); Imperial War Museum 10(B), 15(BL), 16(BR), 19(T),
20(BR), 30(BL); Kobal Collection 34(BR), 35(TL), 35(TR), 35(BR), 41(BL); Peter
Newark's Western Americana 9(T), 24(T); Robert Opie 11(BR); Photo Researchers
Inc 38(T); Popperfoto 6(B), 7(T), 7(B), 8(BL), 8(BR), 11(TR), 11(BL), 12(T), 12(B),
13(T), 13(B), 14(T), 14(C), 14(B), 16(T), 16(BL), 17(TR), 17(B), 18(T), 19(BR),
22(BL), 22(BR), 24(BL), 25(T), 26(T), 27(T), 27(B), 28(B), 30(T), 30(BR), 31(B),
32(T), 34(T), 35(BL), 36(T), 36(BR), 37(CR), 38(BL), 39(TL), 39(BR), 40(T), 40(BL),
42(B); Trustees of the Science Museum 29(TR); Suddeutscher Verlag 20(BL); TRH
9(B), 17(TL), 18(B), 21(B); Tate Gallery: 41(T); Tate Gallery/John Webb 41(C);
Topham 10(T), 21(T), 24(BR), 25(B), 26(B), 32(B), 36(CL), 36(CR), 37(T), 37(B),
38(BR), 39(TR), 39(C), 42(C); Ullstein 6(T), 15(T), 20(T); by courtesy of the Board of
Trustees of the Victoria and Albert Museum 11(TL), 43(C).

cover: Hulton-Deutsch/Popperfoto
frontispiece: Imperial War Museum

# Contents

# Introduction

The decade of the 1940s is dominated by World War II. Until 1945 the world was engaged in the most costly and destructive war in history affecting everybody in various ways. For many people the war years were a desperate struggle for survival as many homes, cities and lives were lost.

Before 1942 it seemed as if victory was impossible. However, when Hitler invaded Russia and later declared war on the United States after the Japanese attack on Pearl Harbor, he over-reached himself. After that, although it was not obvious at the time, his defeat was inevitable and Germany finally surrendered in May 1945, bringing six years of fighting, devastation and loss to an end.

Perhaps the most dramatic result of the war was the sudden confrontation in Europe between the Soviet Union and the United States which changed the face of world politics. Stalin, the "gallant Russian ally" was suddenly seen as a bloody-handed tyrant.

In an astonishing reversal yesterday's enemies were helped to their feet and given the aid they needed to rebuild their countries and regain their places in a world which was now dominated by two "superpowers."

The second half of the decade saw a surprisingly rapid postwar recovery. There had been rapid advances in science, technology and medical knowledge largely the by-products of wartime research and development which now had peacetime applications.

Peace also brought social change as the war undermined old attitudes and replaced them with a new spirit of community. The success of the United Nations organization in dealing with postwar problems such as refugees and food shortages seemed to offer hope for future international cooperation.

# The nature of World War II

In many ways, World War II was a continuation of World War I, fought by almost all of the same contestants and for many of the same reasons.

However, it was much more widespread than before and almost every corner of the world was touched in some way by the fighting and its effects. It also proved to be a great deal more destructive and immensely more cruel than any previous war.

The use of airplanes in support of tanks made it mainly a war of movement. In 1940, the Germans used *blitzkrieg* or "lightning war" to overrun and occupy most of Western Europe with astonishing ease.

While Russia, the United States and Britain led the bitter five year struggle to free the occupied countries from Nazi control, millions of Eastern Europeans were being used by the Nazis as slave labor. Millions of others were put into concentration camps. Probably one quarter of the population of Europe was displaced by the war, either forcibly or as they fled from the enemy.

This was a total war, fought not just by soldiers, sailors and airmen, but also by civilian populations. The long range bombers which pounded factories and destroyed cities, also brought women and children into the front line of battle.

◁ Blitzkrieg! German tanks supported by Stuka dive bombers smashed through the badly equipped Allied armies during the first half of the war. Motorized infantry then rushed through the gaps to mop up the enemy's broken forces.

▽ Threatened by advancing armies and made homeless by the bombing of their cities, millions of people became refugees.

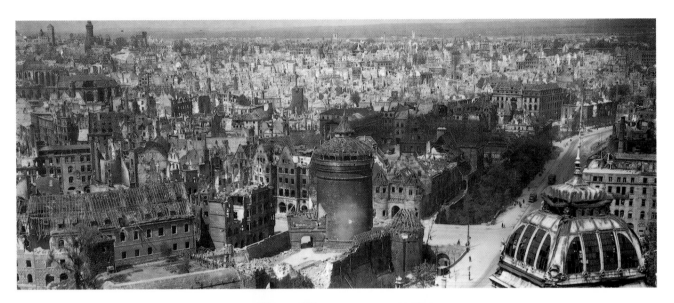

△ Major cities throughout Europe suffered as a result of enemy bombing. Here, amidst the ruins of Nuremberg, Hitler's surviving lieutenants were put on trial in November 1945, accused of crimes against humanity. It was the first trial of its kind and the world was horrified by the evidence of widespread Nazi atrocities.

▷ In this total war, civilians became soldiers. The war was as much won by Air Raid wardens, firemen, women factory workers and children who collected waste paper for the war effort, as it was by members of the armed forces.

# Blitzkrieg!

The "phoney war" ended dramatically in May 1940, when Hitler's tanks burst through Holland and Belgium into France, throwing the Allies into total confusion.

The British army made a miraculous escape from Dunkirk and eight days later France surrendered to the enemy. In order to claim total victory the Nazis only had to win air supremacy while their forces crossed the English Channel. However, in the Battle of Britain, the Royal Air Force (RAF) destroyed so many German planes that Hitler canceled the invasion and attacked the Soviet Union instead.

In December 1941 the Japanese, wanting to seize a rich empire in southeast Asia, tried to neutralize U.S. naval power in the Pacific. Japanese aircraft made a surprise attack on the U.S. Pacific Fleet. Eight battleships and many other smaller ships were torpedoed or bombed. This incident was to prove a turning point in the war.

◁ During the first few days of June 1940, the encircled British army was evacuated from Dunkirk. An armada of small fishing boats and pleasure craft sailed to France to help to rescue the stranded soldiers.

△ On June 14, 1940, the German army entered Paris.

▽ RAF Mosquitos taking off at dawn to attack German shipping off the Norwegian coast. The bomber was the main strike weapon against Nazi-occupied Europe.

▷ On June 22, 1941, Hitler's armies invaded Russia. They made huge advances at first but by December they had been brought to a standstill by General Zhukov and Russia's oldest ally, the winter snows.

▽ On December 7, 1941, without any warning, Japanese planes attacked the U.S. naval base at Pearl Harbor, Hawaii. Within hours the United States, which had been neutral up to this point, declared war on Japan.

# The home front

During the war, whole populations had to be mobilized to help the war effort. Millions of men were conscripted into the armed forces. Women or retired people rushed to take over their jobs in the factories.

To release food for the armed services and Allies, Americans were urged to plant Victory gardens of vegetables. The government organized air raid blackouts, war production and rationing for war materials like gasoline. People were encouraged to collect scrap metals and buy war bonds. Everyone had their job to do.

Civilians also came into the front line in occupied Europe. Millions were used as forced labor or put into concentration camps. In many countries resistance movements were formed to undermine the German occupation.

It was a war that affected nearly everybody in some way.

△ At the outbreak of war, the British government feared that the bombing of large cities would cause millions of casualties. Arrangements were made to evacuate children from the towns to the safety of the countryside. Air raid precautions included a blackout of streets and houses, air raid sirens to warn of approaching bombers and extra emergency services.

◁ There were no deep shelters in London so many people spent the night in underground stations. Several stations were hit by bombs and at least 500 people were killed. However, this did not stop those Londoners who preferred the companionship of the stations to the lonely dampness of their garden shelters.

◁ The Ministry of Food told Britons how to eat wisely.

△ Local Defense Volunteers practice their shooting.

▷ "The Kitchen Front" – a poster advertising 122 wartime recipes which were broadcast on British radio by famous people. This was just one of the many ways in which the Ministry of Food told Britons how to make the best of their rations.

▽ Scrap metal was collected throughout the United States and Britain for the war effort.

11

# Women at war

Women volunteered in the Women's Auxiliary Army Corps and the other services so that men would be freed from clerical and support duties to fight for their country. Millions of men had left their jobs to join the armed forces. Women replaced them in every walk of life, including heavy and dangerous jobs, like working in shipyards and in munitions factories. For many women their war work gave them a wage for the first time, though this did not necessarily compensate them for the long hours and boredom of much of the work. They also had to suffer a good deal of prejudice at first, although this largely died away when they more than proved their worth.

In addition to doing their war work, women also had to deal with the strains and problems of losing their husbands or men friends to the forces.

Daycare centers opened to care for preschool children of working mothers, but household chores still took time and had to be done.

Women proved to be the greatest unused natural resource the country had.

△ Much of the dangerous work in munitions factories was done by women. Here a Merlin engine is being given a final inspection.

◁ The German U-boat campaign caused major food shortages in Britain. As young farm workers joined the forces, thousands of women volunteered for the Land Army to work on the land. Many people were surprised that women could do heavy work like this.

 Women of the ATS operating searchlights. Women worked in every branch of the armed forces. They were nurses, radio operators and worked the rangefinders for anti-aircraft guns. Some flew planes, ferrying them from the factory to the air field. These were dangerous jobs, but only members of the Women's Home Defense Corps were trained to shoot.

▽ These members of the Women's Royal Naval Service (Wrens) are fitting smoke floats to a trainer aircraft of the Fleet Air Army. Women proved themselves not only to be the equal of men, but in many cases they were thought to be better at certain jobs, especially those involving delicate instruments or great concentration. Some died like men as well.

# Triumphs and disasters

Before 1942, the Allies had been defeated on all fronts. The Germans occupied Europe and much of Russia. The Japanese occupied much of Asia.

Then, quite suddenly it seemed, the tide turned. The German invasion of Russia faltered in the face of stubborn Russian resistance.

In North Africa, the British Eighth Army, led by General Montgomery, won a great victory at El Alamein. American forces landed in Tunisia and then, within a few months, 110,000 members of Rommel's Afrika Corps had been taken prisoner.

In July 1943, as a first step toward an invasion of Italy, Allied forces landed on the island of Sicily. Then the United States invaded Salerno and began to advance up the Italian peninsular.

Meanwhile, the Germans were badly defeated at Stalingrad. In Burma, Indian soldiers began to win victories against the Japanese.

In 1942, American marines landed on Guadalcanal Island and reclaimed this Japanese Pacific stronghold.

▽ American Marines landing on Guadalcanal Island in the South Pacific. The six-month battle for Guadalcanal was one of the most vicious campaigns of World War II.

Japanese troops advancing into Burma (top). The capital, Rangoon, fell in March 1942 and main oil-fields were destroyed to prevent them falling into Japanese hands.

△ On February 15, 1942, the Japanese captured the great naval base and fortress of Singapore. It was believed to be impregnable. Its loss was a heavy blow to the Allies.

△ Russian soldiers advancing through the ruins of Stalingrad. The German Sixth Army reduced the city to rubble but failed to capture it. The Russians hung on grimly, and in November 1942, surrounded and defeated the Germans.

△ General Montgomery, commander of the British Eighth Army, looks over El Alamein.

▷ U.S. tanks roll ashore from landing craft during the Allied landing at Anzio, Italy, in May 1944.

# The war at sea

Keeping control of shipping lanes was vital to the Allies. They could not have survived without food and war materials which were brought from abroad by sea – mostly from the United States.

Allied shipping faced the threat of German surface raiders, like the *Graf Spee* and the *Bismarck*, but the most serious danger came from beneath the waves – the German U-boat fleet. It was not until the later part of the war that the U-boats were overcome.

This was largely thanks to the convoy system, where a small number of warships could protect a large number of merchant ships. Fitting ships with radar and sonar underwater detection equipment also helped to defeat the U-boat menace.

In the Pacific, aircraft carriers fought a new kind of long range war where the ships involved were too far apart to see each other. American victories in the Coral Sea, off Midway Island and in the Leyte Gulf destroyed Japanese naval power.

This enabled U.S. forces to "leapfrog" through the Pacific recapturing Japanese-held islands as they went.

▽ The German surface raider *Bismarck* fires at H.M.S. *Hood*. A few minutes later H.M.S. *Hood* was hit and exploded, with the loss of 1,418 lives.

The British navy then hunted down and sank the *Bismarck*. The sailors being picked up were blown off the *Bismarck's* decks during the battle.

◁ Officers of the Royal Navy and RAF Coastal Command in Operations Rooms on shore organizing the movement of ships and planes defending the waters of Britain. Their most vital role was the protection of homecoming convoys.

△ Sailors loading a Grumman Avenger on the deck of the aircraft carrier H.M.S. *Indomitable.*

◁ A Japanese kamikaze pilot, his plane loaded with high explosives, trying to crash onto an American ship.

▽ Hellcat fighters on the deck of H.M.S. *Indomitable* during the attack on Japanese-held oil refineries in Sumatra. The fighters escorted the bomber strike force on its mission but their main task was to defend the carrier from incoming enemy bombers.

# Towards victory

On D-Day, June 6, 1944, ferried by a huge fleet of ships and protected by the largest airforce in the world, Allied forces, under the command of American General Dwight Eisenhower, landed on the coast of Normandy in northern France. The Germans, who had been expecting the invasion to come across the Channel near Calais, hesitated for a few vital days. During this period, the Allied troops successfully completed the largest sea-borne invasion in history and established a powerful bridgehead.

Six weeks later, reinforced by a steady stream of men and equipment, the Allies launched their attack towards Paris.

Caught between this formidable force approaching from the west and the advancing Russians in the east, the Germans fled for their own frontiers. One by one the countries of Europe were liberated. Once the Allies had crossed the Rhine, the Germans soon surrendered and the Nazi regime came to an end.

The Americans, led by General Douglas MacArthur reconquered the Philippines. The war ended soon after the dropping of two atomic bombs on Hiroshima and Nagasaki in August 1945, inflicting great devastation. Within a few weeks, Japan had surrendered.

On August 14, 1945, the most costly and bloody war ever fought, finally came to an end and Europe was left to pick up the pieces.

△ French tanks being welcomed by civilians near Paris. Paris was liberated on August 25, 1944.

▽ American soldiers help to drag survivors ashore after their landing craft had sunk during the D-day landings.

▷ It was not until March 1945 that the Allies managed to cross the Rhine, Germany's formidable Western border. The Germans were trapped between two overwhelming forces and their resistance finally crumbled. On April 25, 1945, American soldiers advancing from the West met Russian soldiers advancing from the East on the banks of the River Elbe, south of Berlin. Five days later, trapped amidst the blazing ruins of his capital city in his underground bunker, and unable to face capture, Hitler committed suicide. On May 7, the German forces surrendered and the Nazi empire which Hitler had boasted would last for a thousand years, came to an end. The Allies could then turn their full energies toward victory against Japan.

▽ The devastation of Hiroshima after the explosion of the atomic bomb. Many have criticized the dropping of the bomb, pointing out that Japan was already near collapse, her people starving and her industry ruined. Others have said that the final defeat of Japan would have cost millions of Allied lives.

△ American soldiers digging in on the beaches of Leyte Island. The United States reconquest of the Pacific islands put a stranglehold on Japan.

# Cleaning up Europe

After the end of the war, enormous problems, social and economic, were brought to light. About 50 million people had been killed and large areas of Europe had been laid waste by the fighting. Millions of refugees needed to be resettled, fed and clothed. The United States' government put forward the Marshall Plan to help to pay for the recovery of Europe.

In Germany, a de-Nazification program was put into operation. Non-Nazis were placed in important positions and Nazi leaders were tried for "war crimes."

As an added complication to this situation, the Soviet Union refused to give up the lands which she occupied in eastern Europe. The United States' government was not prepared to stand by while a large part of Europe became communist. So, in 1947, President Truman announced that the United States would resist any further extension of communism into Europe. The United States and the Soviet Union, the former wartime Allies, now found themselves in opposing camps.

△ Berlin, reduced to rubble by Allied bombing, was divided into four zones. The Western Allies created a democratic government in Germany to replace Nazi dictatorship and helped German industries to recover.

▽ The full horror of the Nazi regime was revealed when the concentration camps were opened up. These slave laborers at Buchenwald Camp survived. Millions of others, men, women and children, did not.

△ Millions of Germans fled from the advancing Russians, preferring to surrender to the British, Americans or French. When the war ended and Germany was divided into four zones of occupation, many Germans refused to return to their homes in the Russian sector but were forced to do so by the Western Allies.

△ Berlin lay deep within the Russian zone. In 1948, Stalin tried to persuade Berliners to join the Soviet sector by blocking routes into the city. The Western Allies responded by airlifting in supplies.

▷ At the Yalta Conference in February 1945, the Allied leaders agreed how Germany would be smashed, divided and punished, and how Europe would be rehabilitated. However, this was the last time the war leaders met. Shortly afterwards, Churchill lost power in a general election and Roosevelt died. East-West relations soon worsened as Russia drew an "Iron Curtain" across the frontiers of the lands she occupied and refused to allow free elections to be held in Eastern Europe. The "Cold War" had begun.

# Post-war United States

Troop ships returned millions of G.I.'s to the United States, eager to make up for lost time. With money they had saved during the war, Americans wanted to go on a spending spree, but industries could not convert to peacetime production instantaneously. Housing was hard to find. There were shortages of autos, household appliances, and food so prices soared.

Strikes troubled the economy as workers demanded higher wages to keep up with rising prices. The government removed wartime economic controls but restricted work stoppages. Under government programs, many G.I.'s went back to school. Others took civilian jobs while women readjusted to being wives and homemakers. Blacks, who flocked to northern cities for wartime factory work, sought equal rights as American citizens.

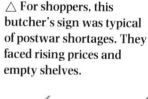
no meat prices doubled since yesterday we refuse to handle

△ For shoppers, this butcher's sign was typical of postwar shortages. They faced rising prices and empty shelves.

▽ Soldiers, marines, WACs and WAVEs celebrating VE day on Broadway.

▷U.S. bomber crews returning on a troop ship to the States.

▷ In 1948, members of the United Mine Workers union went on strike for higher pay. The strike turned violent when nonunion workers were hired to keep the coal mines going, shown here standing guard with shotguns. Union members resented the coal companies for replacing them with outsiders.

◁ In 1944, the Serviceman's Readjustment Act, or "G.I. Bill of Rights" as it was more popularly known, was passed. This provided a great deal of practical help and training for servicemen wanting to readjust to civilian life.

▷ Quonset huts, the fast answer to a housing shortage, were shaped like half cylinders and were made of corrugated steel. They usually housed two families, one at each end.

# A changed world: the Far East

Japan surrendered shortly after atomic bombs were dropped on Hiroshima and Nagasaki by the United States' Air Force in August 1945. Japan was then occupied by American troops, given economic aid and educated to become a democracy.

The Americans willingly granted the Philippines independence. Although the French tried to hold on to Vietnam and the Dutch tried to retain the Dutch East Indies, it was to no avail as, along with the British, they found their empires melting away.

In China the corrupt Nationalist regime of Chiang Kai-Shek was swept away and replaced, in 1949, by the Communist People's Republic of China led by Mao Tse Tung.

△ Mao Tse Tung, leader of the Chinese Communists. He created a peasant militia and taught them the principles of guerilla warfare which they used to fight the Japanese from 1937 to 1945.

◁ Indian machine gunners on Pagoda Hill during the battle of Fort Dufferin. The Japanese put up a fanatical, suicidal resistance before being overcome by the Fourteenth Army, led by General Sir William Slim.

▽ The British flag hoisted at Fort Dufferin in March 1945. The fort was one of the main Japanese strongholds in Mandalay. Its capture broke the Japanese forces and opened the gateway for the Allies to push toward Rangoon, the capital of Burma. The country became independent three years later.

◁ President Chiang Kai-Shek at a final parade just before he left the mainland in 1949 to set up Nationalist China on the island of Formosa.

▷ Ho Chi Minh (second from the left) the leader of the Vietnamese Communist Party was elected President of the Democratic Republic of Vietnam in December 1946. Within a few months he was leading an armed struggle for independence from the French.

# India and Israel

India played a vital part in the war, providing supplies and raising an army of two million men. However, in return for this, Indian leaders demanded independence. In 1947, Lord Mountbatten was appointed viceroy to oversee this process. Mountbatten decided to partition the country to satisfy the Muslims who wanted their own separate state of Pakistan apart from Hindu India.

As independence day approached in August 1947, Muslims fled from India and Hindus fled from Pakistan. In the confusion there were riots and massacres. Nearly half a million people were killed.

After their persecution under the Nazis, the Jews were determined to found their own national state. They chose Palestine, the biblical home of the Jews which had been controlled by the British since 1917. As Jewish immigrants flooded in after 1945, the Arabs living there strongly objected. The British, who found themselves caught between Arab and Israeli guerilla forces, withdrew.

The declaration of the Jewish state of Israel on May 14, 1948 brought immediate recognition by the United States and vast amounts of economic and military aid. Israel repulsed attacks by Egypt and Jordan.

By 1949, the Arabs and Israelis were living in uneasy peace.

◁ Mountbatten and Nehru, who became the first Prime Minister of India, holding discussions. Nehru wanted to make India into a powerful modern state. However, the world's largest democracy faced many economic and political problems.

▽ Tear gas being used against Muslim demonstrators in Lahore. One of the victims of these racial and religious tensions was Mahatma Gandhi, who was assassinated by a Hindu fanatic in 1948.

△ Jewish soldiers fighting Jordan's crack Arab legion during the siege of Jerusalem. There was heavy fighting in the holy city, during which the United Nations mediator was killed by Israeli soldiers. However, the 30,000-strong Israeli army, the Haganah, proved more than a match for the Arabs. They not only repelled the attacks but also advanced to occupy Arab territory. Eventually a truce was signed in 1949.

▷ Jewish immigrants arriving in Israel. The Israeli victory in 1948 led to a great increase in the number of Jews immigrating to the new nation. They set to work with great energy and imagination to make the "desert blossom." However, their arrival underlined the fact that nearly 400,000 Palestinian Arabs were now refugees from their former homes. Their desire to return to their homeland was to cause great problems in the future.

# Science and technology

The need to win the war stimulated research and development in many scientific fields during the first half of the decade. Many of the discoveries concerned weapons, such as the development of rockets by the Germans and the building of the first atomic bomb by the United States. However, some of this research had peacetime applications.

Work with radar and radio helped to develop new electronic equipment, such as transistors, which were invented in 1947 and used in computers and televisions after the war. The development of the jet engine proceeded at a great pace. The sound barrier was broken in 1947 and the first commercial jet airliner flew in 1949.

In 1944, American Oswald Avery discovered that inherited characteristics were passed on through an acid called DNA which carried the genetic information needed by most living cells. Two years later events like these could be recorded with the first ballpoint pens.

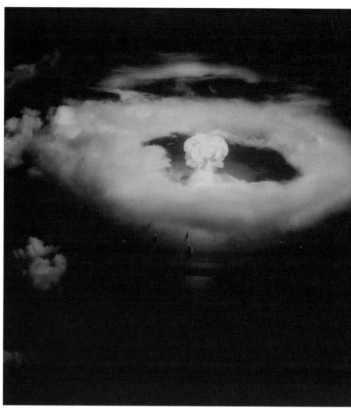

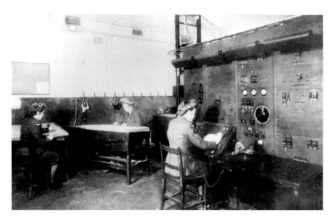

△ Radar, which came to be a key weapon, being used to detect approaching enemy bombers in the war.

▷ The ballpoint pen was invented by a Hungarian journalist, Laszlo Biro, in 1938. It first went on sale in November 1946.

◁ An American atomic bomb test at Bikini Atoll in the Pacific on July 1, 1946.

◁ A magic eye camera gives a sequence of shots of the V-2 rocket. The rocket, used to attack Britain in 1945, flew at the speed of sound.

▷ The computer was developed shortly after the war. Known as "electronic brains," they were much bigger and slower than modern machines. Computers were used to calculate wages. The information is typed in code on to a tape which is then fed into the machine.

BALL POINT PEN

Presented by Miles Martin
Pen Co. Ltd.

In 1888 there is mention of a ball point pen, but the now familiar design is derived from that patented 1938 by Laszlo Biro for a pen filled with a viscous quick drying material fed to a ball point by means of a spring loaded plunger.

For quantity production, instead of a large ink reservoir with spring plunger feed, a long length of copper tubing doubled on itself four times was adopted, the ink being fed to the ball point by capillary action alone.

In the latest models, the copper tubing has been replaced by an acetate tube, of slightly larger bore bent double to form a U, thereby reducing the weight and bulk.

Reference:- Journal of the Society of Arts. Oct. Nov. 1905. British Patent No. 498997. 15th June 1938.

Inv. 1949-174.

# Medicine

The war forced great advances in medicine and surgery. Allied research into nutrition led to synthetic vitamins and dehydrated food packets, called K-rations, ensuring that soldiers had balanced diets. The need to treat large numbers of wounded servicemen led to significant advances in blood transfusion services, plastic surgery, artificial limbs, and antibiotics. These developments continued after the war and helped greatly to improve medical treatment throughout the rest of the decade.

Throughout the decade, epidemics of polio killed hundreds of children and crippled many more. Since vaccines were not yet discovered, Sister Kenny and others tried various treatments to aid victims of this disease. As the postwar birth rate soared, parents consulted pediatrician Benjamin Spock's newly published *Baby and Child Care* to learn how to raise healthier children.

▽ A child being innoculated against diphtheria. Innoculation campaigns became common in the war and were continued afterwards. As a result certain diseases like diphtheria and malaria were virtually wiped out in Europe. This was an important step towards the idea that disease could be prevented rather than simply cured.

△ Sir Alexander Fleming, discoverer of the first antibiotic, penicillin. It was particularly useful for treating wounded soldiers. Other antibiotics like streptomycin and neomycin were discovered during the 1940s.

▽ WACs and enlisted men donating blood to the American Red Cross. During the war the American Red Cross organized a massive and efficient blood bank which saved many lives.

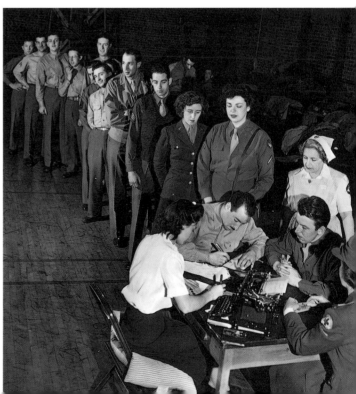

▷ Many servicemen were so badly wounded in the war that it would have been impossible for them to lead normal lives afterwards without special treatment. One of the most important jobs of wartime medical staff was the rehabilitation of wounded soldiers to enable them to lead useful and happy lives. The most modern treatments were used to help them. Servicemen who had lost limbs were fitted with artificial ones and followed courses of occupational therapy to improve their co-ordination. Those with disfiguring wounds received plastic surgery followed by make-up courses to help them disguise their scars. Other forms of treatment included radium and X-ray therapy.

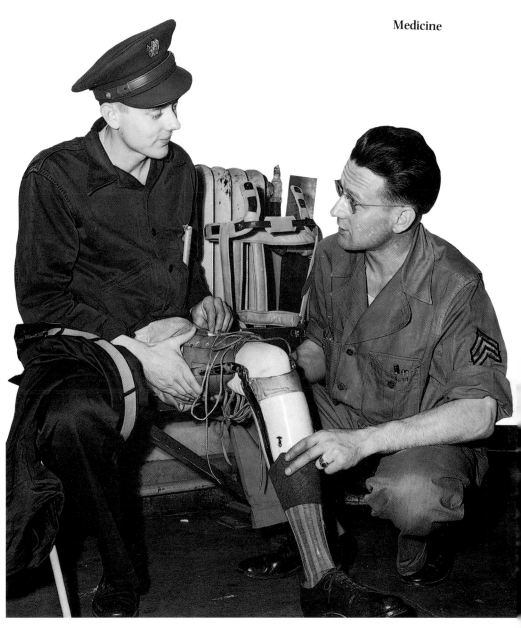

◁ Scientists are seen here working with vitamins. Food shortages during the war led to serious studies of nutrition and diet. As a result, although there was less food, people were better fed and healthier than ever before.

# Fashion

During the war, fashion reflected the need for practical garments suitable for war work. Men mainly wore uniforms. Women wore easy-fitting, plain clothes with square military shoulders.

With shortages of cloth, rationing was introduced and frivolity frowned on. Decorative details like trouser cuffs and pocket flaps disappeared and plain and practical outfits took their place. Skirt hemlines rose to save fabric. For teenage girls, bobby socks and saddle shoes became the latest fad along with blue jeans. Men's hair was cropped short while women wore long hair.

After the war, women were delighted by a return to more elegant fashions when the French designer, Christian Dior, introduced his "New Look" in 1947, which brought back a more feminine shape and style to women's clothes.

△ During the war people could buy plain "utility" clothing.

(Top) Measuring the length of a "New Look" utility dress.

◁ Discharged British airmen, wearing their "demob" suits, cheerfully back to "civvy street."

Alluring...Enduring...

Wolsey
nylons

*Wolsey Limited Leicester*

◁ Nylon lingerie in 1949. Nylon goods gradually made their way into the stores after the war but remained very scarce.

▽ An extract from a mail order catalog of 1943. Wartime shoes were designed for comfort and durability rather than for elegance.

WARDS SHOES FOR COMFORT

**DUTCH TOE**
A Shoe that will go with any outfit. Made on the Dutch Toe last with good strong leather sole and heel. Sizes: 3, 4, 5, 6, 7.
No. G36/603   Black, trimmed Red
No. G36/604   Brown, trimmed Green
Pair   **14'7**
7d. extra for carriage.

**ELABORATE INSTEP TIE**
With special wide fitting lines and comfortable leather heel. Sizes: 3, 4, 5, 6, 7, 8.
No. G36/455   Black.
No. G36/456   Tan................Pair   **25'4**
7d. extra for carriage.

▽ Many clothes in wartime Britain could only be bought with clothing coupons. Each adult had 48 coupons a year.

New and flattering BARGAINS

**FASHIONABLE JACKET STYLE**
Keeps you warm on cold days. Collarless style with two attractively stitched pockets. Fastens down front with self covered buttons. Long sleeves. Warm but light. Padded shoulders. Shaped back. In Scarlet. Women's size. (5 Coupons)
No. E26/765.................... **19'6**

**WARDS FOR EASIEST TERMS**

| Value of Monthly Order Payment | | Value of Monthly Order Payment | |
|---|---|---|---|
| Up to £1 | 3/- | £2/10/- | 7/6 |
| £1/5/- | 4/- | £3 | 9/- |
| £1/10/- | 5/- | £3/10/- | 10/- |

**TAILORED SHIRT STYLE**
In a soft and comfortable Fibro material which resembles shantung. Long sleeves. Breast pocket with inverted pleat. Inverted pleat down back. Wear with slacks or skirt. Colour: Shan-

**SPOTTED FIBRO**
Soft and warm is this long sleeved Blouse. Buttons all down front. Yoke across back, and inverted pleat. Colours: Red and

# Theater and cinema

Broadway theatergoers could enjoy a wide range of dramas and musicals. Tennessee Williams's *Glass Menagerie* and *A Streetcar Named Desire* and Arthur Miller's *Death of a Salesman* attracted serious audiences. The songwriting team of Richard Rodgers and Oscar Hammerstein produced one hit show after another, starting with *Oklahoma*.

During the war, Hollywood offered Americans inspiring war dramas as well as escapist fare. Postwar film *The Best Years of Our Lives* dealt with the problems of returning veterans and their families.

Drive-in movie theaters became popular as more and more people bought cars.

◁ Lee J. Cobb as Willy Loman in a performance of *Death of a Salesman* at the Morosco Theater, New York in 1949. This play by Arthur Miller is about an ordinary man betrayed by the hollow values which are all he knows.

△ Laurence Olivier as *Henry V*. This film, starring Olivier and also directed by him, was shot in Ireland and released in 1944. At that time it was the most expensive film ever made. It was dedicated to those who led the D-Day attack.

▽ Charlie Chaplin in the film *The Great Dictator* (1940). This "withering satire" on Hitler, came too late to amuse Blitz-torn London.

◁ *Casablanca* was released shortly before Churchill and Roosevelt met at the Casablanca Conference in 1943.

△ *The Best Years of Our Lives* was about the resettlement of an ex-serviceman in 1946.

▽ The Marx Brothers were a family of zany American comedians.

▽ Walt Disney, pioneer of full length color cartoon movies. During the war he produced *Fantasia*, *Pinocchio* and *Dumbo*. Scenes which lasted 8 minutes on screen took up to 6 months to produce.

# Sports

During the war years, American sports teams suffered a manpower shortage owing to the call-up of players. Major league baseball continued to be the nation's pastime, but vacancies on the teams were filled by older men.

Postwar American football fans were thrilled by the performance of "Mr. Inside and Mr. Outside," West Point's Glenn Davis and Doc Blanchard. Woman golfer Babe Didrikson Zaharias won honors as an outstanding athlete. Brooklyn Dodger Jackie Robinson became the first black major league baseball player. The National Basketball Association was formed as the decade drew to a close.

△ The 1948 Olympic games held in London and known as the "austerity Olympics" were the first to be held since Hitler's 1936 Nazi propaganda spectacular in Berlin.

▷ Medals struck for the 1948 Olympics were made from oxydized silver instead of the customary gold.

△ Fanny Blankers-Koen, the "Flying Dutchwoman" won 4 medals all for track events, although she was also the world record holder for the high jump.

◁ Triple Crown winner Citation, shown here at the Kentucky Derby, won 19 of his 20 races in 1948.

▷ In 1947, the great Jackie Robinson led the National League in stolen bases. He was named Rookie of the Year. In 1949, he was voted the National League's Most Valuable Player.

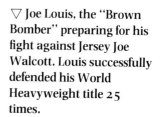

◁ Ben Hogan, in play during the Los Angeles Open Golf Tournament at Santa Monica, California.

▽ Joe Louis, the "Brown Bomber" preparing for his fight against Jersey Joe Walcott. Louis successfully defended his World Heavyweight title 25 times.

◁ Louise Brough playing in the Wimbledon ladies singles final in 1949. She won the title for the third successive time and then for a fourth time in 1955.

# Popular pastimes

Most Americans followed the progress of World War II on their radios by listening to overseas reporters and home front commentators. Comedy shows, game shows, and soap operas were popular programs. Overseas troops tuned in to Armed Forces Radio. Local canteens and traveling USO shows entertained them.

Americans liked to listen and dance to the music of the Big Bands. Benny Goodman, the Dorsey brothers, and Glenn Miller's orchestra drew large crowds as did Bing Crosby and Frank Sinatra. The Andrews Sisters and other popular singing groups were juke box favorites.

Postwar Americans collected LP records and watched comedian Milton Berle or Western hero "Hopalong Cassidy" on their new television sets. Bubblegum, rubber balls and metal toys delighted children once again.

△ During the war, television broadcasting was suspended. In 1945, the national networks, all based in New York, began broadcasting again. At first the services reached only between Boston and Washington D.C. However, a boom soon developed and by the end of the decade, over six million homes had television sets.

◁ Open air concerts provided welcome relief for the troops at the front.

◁ (Inset) Vera Lynn, the "Forces Sweetheart." She received a thousand requests a week to sing favorites like *We'll Meet Again* on the radio. Amazingly the War Office and BBC thought the sentimental lyrics would sap the men's fighting spirit.

△ The *Jitterbug* became an immediate craze. Energetic dancing was a great outlet for frayed nerves and boredom.

▽ In Britain, resorts were closed during the war and beaches covered with defenses. However, once the mines and wire were cleared after 1945, it was business as usual.

△ The great Glenn Miller. He spent six months in Britain giving concerts before he was lost in a plane crash in 1944. His tune *In the Mood* was one of the best-loved of the war years.

△ An ATS band (top) in full swing. Each service had its own bands. The RAF *Squadronaires* were the best known, but the Army had its *Blue Rockets* and the Navy its *Blue Mariners*.

# The arts

During the war, while G.I.'s decorated their barracks with photos of pin-up girls, priceless European art treasures were shipped to the United States for safekeeping. Artist Norman Rockwell focused on traditional American themes in his work. Postwar architects submitted starkly modern designs for buildings, and abstract expressionist painting, started in the early forties, became popular.

During the war, American composer Aaron Copland's music reflected on the nation's past. Many noted European composers, such as Bartok and Stravinsky, sought refuge in the United States, enabling American concert-goers to become more familiar with their works. Postwar audiences enjoyed new operas written by Gian-Carlo Menotti as well as works by Leonard Barnstein.

During the war, Americans scrambled to read Kathleen Windsor's racy *Forever Amber* and Hemingway's classic *For Whom the Bell Tolls*. Postwar novelists such as Norman Mailer, Irwin Shaw and James Michener described wartime experiences in their books.

▽ **Author Ernest Hemingway used his experiences as a war correspondent to provide vivid backgrounds for his stories.**

△ **T.S. Eliot (center), a much honored poet and playwright. Like Hemingway he won a Nobel prize for literature.**

◁ George Orwell, author of *1984* and *Animal Farm*. His books contain powerful social comments which were not usually well received at the time.

▽ *The Dead Sea* by Paul Nash. As a war artist he used his surrealistic style to produce haunting pictures. This one is part of a group which records the Battle of Britain.

▷ Pen drawing by Henry Moore, *Tube shelter perspective*. Moore was a war artist for two years, and he was also probably the most important 20th century sculptor.

▽ Benjamin Britten working on his opera *Peter Grimes*. His many pieces for children included *The Young Person's Guide to the Orchestra*.

▷ Moira Shearer putting on the red shoes she wore in the film of the same name. It won an Oscar in the 1949 American Academy awards.

# Toward a better world

By the late 1940s, in spite of the hostility between East and West, the world was making a good recovery. Generous aid from the United States helped Europe recover from some of the worst effects of the war. President Harry Truman offered underdeveloped nations the Point Four program of technical assistance to raise their people's living standards.

There was also a new spirit of international co-operation. The Organization of European Economic Cooperation sought to increase European prosperity. The Organization of American States pledged mutual assistance among Western Hemisphere nations. The founding of the United Nations offered a new hope for the future.

△ The 12 member nations signing the Atlantic Treaty in Washington DC in 1949. NATO (the North Atlantic Treaty Organization) was set up to protect Europe from the new "Red Menace" in Eastern Europe.

◁ The first cargo of American aid under the Marshall Plan reaches Britain. The Minister of Food, John Strachey, watches the unloading with the ship's captain.

▷ The opening session of the United Nations assembly in the Palais de Chaillot, Paris, in 1948. It was hoped that the UN would help nations to solve their disputes peacefully in the future. The UN also set up many agencies, such as UNICEF and other relief organizations which distributed money, food and medical supplies to war-stricken countries.

▷ Unlike the situation in most countries, the American way of life seemed almost untouched by the effects of the war. In 1945, America was left as the only rich country. It was largely the wealth and generosity of the United States which enabled the world to recover as quickly as it did.

△ The caption reads "With the Marshall Plan inter-European co-operation for a higher standard of living." The Marshall Plan provided over $13 billion to help Europe to recover from the effects of the war. Stalin refused the aid and believed the Plan to be an American attempt to dominate Europe. Well-organized postwar relief programs prevented famine, epidemics and catastrophic upheavals.

▷ The window dresser in Gamages department store hurries to show that certain items of clothing have come off the ration in January 1949. Rationing did not end altogether in Britain until 1953.

# Personalities of the 1940s

**Bernstein, Leonard** (1918–90), American composer who made his conducting debut in 1943 upon the sudden illness of Bruno Walter and went on to write symphonic works and show music.

**Chaplin, Sir Charles** (1889–1977), known as Charlie. English film actor and director, considered by many to be the greatest star of silent movies. Best known for his slapstick comedy routines.

**Chiang Kai-Shek** (1887–1975), Chinese general and one of the "Big Four" war leaders. Defeated by the Communists, (1949), he retreated from the mainland and founded "National" China on the island of Formosa (Taiwan).

**Churchill, Winston** (1874–1965), As Prime Minister and Minister of Defense from 1940 to 1945, he led and inspired the British people from Dunkirk to the surrender of Germany. His government was defeated by Labor in the 1945 election, but he was again Prime Minister from 1951–1955.

**Copland, Aaron** (1900–90), American composer of symphonies incorporating jazz and folk elements.

**Crosby, Bing** (1904–77), American crooner, nicknamed the "Old Groaner," whose melodious voice made him the most popular singer of all time.

**Eisenhower, Dwight** (1890–1969), American general, Supreme Commander of Allied Forces in Europe 1944–45. Blessed with inexhaustible patience and tact, "Ike" also possessed the priceless gift of being able to get Allied commanders to work together for victory. In 1953, he became President of the United States.

**Eliot, Thomas Stearns** (1888–1965), American poet, critic and playwright. He became a British subject in 1927. His most famous plays included *Murder in the Cathedral* and *The Family Reunion*. *Old Possum's Book of Practical Cats* has become a classic verse collection.

**Goering, Herman** (1893–1946), A leading Nazi, this former fighter ace, commanded the German *Luftwaffe* throughout World War II, although his greed and laziness made him increasingly unpopular. Sentenced to death for war crimes, he took poison in his cell at Nuremburg.

**Hitler, Adolf** (1889–1945), Austrian megalomaniac who founded the German Nazi party and became Fuhrer of Germany. From 1939 to 1941, his armies overran most of Europe; he then attacked Russia, almost achieving total victory. However, the tide turned against him in 1942 after which there were only major defeats and stubborn retreat.

**Mountbatten, Louis** (1900–79), British admiral, chief of Combined Operations 1942, Supreme Allied Commander South East Asia 1943–45. Last Viceroy of India and India's first Governor-General, 1947–48.

**Mussolini, Benito** (1883–1945), Italian dictator and Hitler's closest ally, until the feeble performance of Italy's forces reduced him to a mere lackey. He was shot by his own countrymen when attempting to flee to Switzerland.

**Nehru, Pandit Jawaharlal** (1889–1964), Prime Minister of India, 1947–64. In spite of years in prison for opposing British rule, Nehru was a strong supporter of the Commonwealth. For India, he worked to improve industry, farming and social welfare.

**Nimitz, Chester** (1885–1966), American admiral who commanded U.S. naval forces in the Pacific throughout the war and contributed greatly to the defeat of Japan.

**Patton, George Smith** (1885–1945), American general, a specialist in tank warfare whose daring, even reckless, advances earned him the nickname "Old Blood and Guts."

Winston Churchill

Dwight Eisenhower

Adolf Hitler

**Robinson, Jack** (1919–1972), American baseball player who was the first black on a major league team. He played for the Brooklyn Dodgers from 1947–56.

**Rodgers, Richard** (1902–79), American songwriter. He worked with Lorenz Hart and Oscar Hammerstein to produce some of the best-loved musicals ever written. With Hammerstein he wrote, among others, *Oklahoma* and *South Pacific*.

**Rommel, Erwin** (1891–1944), German general and master of desert warfare whom Montgomery defeated at El Alamein. Rommel commanded the German forces which opposed the Allied invasion of Normandy. He committed suicide after the failure of a German army plot to assassinate Hitler.

**Roosevelt, Franklin Delano** (1882–1945), President of the United States 1933–45. Before Pearl Harbor, he supported the Allied cause and formed a close understanding with Churchill and, later, with Stalin. His mistakes have been much criticized, but by his actions he saved Britain and much of Europe from the horrors of Nazi domination.

**Sinatra, Frank** (1915–1998), American singer, actor, and composer, who reached stardom in the 1940s: he roused his fans to screaming pitch.

**Stalin, Josef** (1879–1953), Russian leader, from 1924 to 1953, who joined Hitler in crushing Poland and then accepted Allied aid after Germans attacked Russia. He never relaxed his hostility to the West, and made it his policy to bring the whole of eastern Europe under Soviet control.

**Tito, Josip Broz (Marshall)** (1892–1980), President of Yugoslavia, who led the partisans so well against the occupying Germans that he was able to form a Communist government after the war and even to defy Stalin.

**Tojo, Hideki** (1884–1948), Japanese general and Prime Minister who urged close collaboration with Germany and authorized the attack on Pearl Harbor. After the war he was hanged for major war crimes.

**Truman, Harry** (1884–1972), American President, 1945–53, who succeeded Roosevelt and made the decision to use atomic bombs against Japan. Later the "Truman Doctrine" promised American aid to any free nation resisting Communist pressure.

**Vandenberg, Arthur Hendrick** (1884–1951), United States Republican senator who was the architect of postwar bipartisan foreign policy of active participation in the United Nations.

**Williams, Tennesee** (Thomas Lanier) (1914–88), renowned American playright who explored society's frustrations in dramas filled with tensions.

**Zaharias, Babe (Mildred) Didrikson** (1913–56), outstanding American all-round women's athlete who became a champion golfer during the 1940s.

Douglas MacArthur

Franklin D. Roosevelt

Josef Stalin

# 1940s year by year

## 1940

- Germany invades Denmark and Norway.
- Churchill becomes Prime Minister.
- German armies invade Holland, Belgium and France.
- British army evacuated from Dunkirk.
- Germans take Paris.
- Italy enters the war.
- France capitulates.
- Battle of Britain: the RAF defeats the Luftwaffe.
- The German-Italian-Japanese Pact.
- Germany steps up U-boat attacks.
- U.S. Congress approves a vast expansion of the U.S. army and navy.
- Roosevelt re-elected President.
- Sikorsky helicopter flies in the United States.
- Duke Ellington plays jazz.
- First electron microscope demonstrated in the United States.
- Ernest Hemingway writes *For Whom the Bell Tolls*.

## 1941

- Roosevelt signs Lend Lease Act.
- Germans overrun Yugoslavia, Greece and Crete.
- Malta bombed.
- German battleship *Bismarck* sunk.
- Germans invade Russia and reach the outskirts of Leningrad and Moscow.
- Churchill and Roosevelt meet to sign the Atlantic Charter.
- Japanese planes bomb Pearl Harbor.
- Japan attacks the Philippines.
- United States declares war on Japan, Germany and Italy.
- *Citizen Kane* opens.
- Japanese capture Guam, Wake Island and Hong Kong.
- Price controls begin in the United States.

## 1942

- Japanese invade Burma, Malaya, the Dutch East Indies and capture Rangoon, Singapore and Bataan.
- First U.S. bomber raid on Tokyo.
- Rommel captures Tobruk in North Africa.
- U.S. Navy wins vital battles of the Coral Sea and Midway Island.
- Germans surrounded at Stalingrad.
- Montgomery's eighth Army defeats Rommel at El Alamein. Rommel retreats.
- American and British troops land in French North Africa.
- U.S. marines take Guadalcanal. MacArthur begins "island hopping."
- Gandhi demands that the British should "Quit India."
- First electronic computer is built.
- Sugar, coffee and gasoline rationed in the United States.
- Bing Crosby croons "White Christmas." Other popular songs are "Paper Doll' and "That Old Black Magic."
- Enrico Fermi splits the atom in the United States.

## 1943

- Churchill and Roosevelt meet at Casablanca in North Africa.
- Germans surrender at Stalingrad.
- Russians recover city after city as they drive the enemy westwards.
- Allies carry out day and night bombing of Germany.
- RAF bomb Berlin.
- Mussolini overthrown. Italy joins the Allies.
- Roosevelt, Churchill and Stalin meet at Tehran.
- U.S. forces continue island-hopping towards the Philippines.
- H.M.S. *Duke of York* sinks German battlecruiser *Scharnhorst* in Atlantic.
- Penicillin saves many lives.
- American 10,000 ton Liberty ships are said to be built in 4 days.
- *Oklahoma* takes New York by storm.
- Jitterbug dancing is all the rage.
- United States rations shoes, then meat, cheese, canned goods.

## 1944

- Americans recapture islands in the Pacific.
- D-Day landings in Normandy.
- July Plot by Army officers fails to kill Hitler.
- Polish uprising in Warsaw crushed by the Germans.
- Allies invade southern France.
- Allies enter Paris, Brussels and Antwerp.
- V2 rockets bombard London.
- Allied advance checked by German successes at Arnhem and in the Ardennes.
- U.S. troops invade Philippines.
- Japanese navy decisively beaten in the battle of the Leyte Gulf.
- Roosevelt is elected to fourth term as U.S. president.
- Ho Chi Minh declares Vietnam's independence from France.
- Aaron Copland composes "Appalachian Spring."

## 1945

- Churchill, Roosevelt and Stalin meet at Yalta.
- U.S. troops capture Manila and Okinawa, only 560 km (350 miles) from Japan.
- Allied forces cross the river Rhine into Germany.
- Mussolini killed by Italian partisans.
- Hitler commits suicide.
- British forces recapture Rangoon.
- Roosevelt dies and is succeeded by Harry Truman.
- Germany surrenders.
- Victory in Europe (V.E. day).
- United Nations Charter signed.
- U.S. planes bomb Japan.
- Truman, Stalin and Attlee meet at

Potsdam.
- De Gaulle elected as President of France.
- Atomic bomb destroys Hiroshima.
- Japan surrenders.
- World War II ends.
- Civil war breaks out in China.
- Tito becomes head of Yugoslavia.
- Orwell's novel *Animal Farm* published.
- International Bank for Reconstruction and Development is founded.

# 1946

- The first session of the UN General Assembly opens in London. Paul Spaak of Belgium becomes the first president.
- Germany divided into four occupation zones. Berlin divided into four sectors.
- Churchill makes his Iron Curtain speech in Fulton, Missouri.
- Peace Conference held in Paris.
- The United States and Britain merge their occupation zones in Germany.
- Truman approves a loan to Britain.
- Verdict given in Nuremberg trial of Nazi leaders.
- U.S. navy explodes underwater atomic bomb at Bikini.
- UNESCO (United Nations Economic and Social Council) founded.
- Electronic brain built in the United States.
- The musical *Annie Get Your Gun* opens in New York.
- Benjamin Spock's *Baby and Child Care* is published.
- Joe Louis wins his 23rd defense of the world heavy-weight title.
- *The Best Years of Our Lives* opens in movie theaters.
- Xerography process invented.

# 1947

- Marshall Plan announced to aid

European recovery.
- Burma chooses independence.
- India divided into two dominions: India (Hindu) and Pakistan (Muslim).
- Truman sets up loyalty-security program for government employees.
- Brooklyn Dodger Jackie Robinson becomes the first black to play major league baseball.
- "New Look" fashions arrive.
- Chuck Yeager, in a Bell X-1 rocket plane, reached a speed of over 600 mph, breaking the sound barrier.
- First "flying saucers" reported.
- *Kon-Tiki* raft sailed from Peru to Polynesia.

# 1948

- Gandhi assassinated by a Hindu fanatic in India.
- Berlin airlift begins.
- Jewish state of Israel proclaimed.
- World Health Organization founded.
- South Africa adopts apartheid.
- Transistors and long-playing records are invented in the United States.
- The Organization of European Economic Cooperation (OEEC), the forerunner of the European Common Market, is founded.
- Rocket missiles tested in the United States.
- North Korea declares itself to be a republic under Kim Il Sung. Hopes of reuniting North and South Korea fade.
- Truman elected President of the United States.
- Ben Hogan wins U.S. Open golf championship.
- Truman orders an end to racial segregation in the American armed services.
- Olivier's film of *Hamlet* released.
- At the Olympic Games which are held in London, the Dutch athlete Fanny Blankers-Koen wins four gold medals.
- Norman Mailer's war novel, *The*

*Naked and the Dead* is published.
- The UN adopts Declataion of Human Rights.

# 1949

- Truman proposes Point Four program of technical assistance to underdeveloped nations.
- Twelve nations sign a treaty setting up the North Atlantic Treaty Organization (NATO).
- Council of Europe is established.
- Indonesia declares her independence.
- France grants independence to Vietnam.
- Adenauer becomes the first Chancellor of the German Federal Republic (West Germany).
- Russia lifts the Berlin blockade and establishes the German Democratic Republic (East Germany) in the Soviet zone.
- Nehru becomes Prime Minster of India.
- Arab-Israeli armistice. Jerusalem is partitioned between Israel and Jordan.
- People's Republic of China proclaimed under Mao Tse Tung. Chiang Kai-Shek sets up Nationalist China on the island of Formosa.
- The Soviet Union tests its first atomic bomb.
- Bikini bathing suits appear in the United States.
- First jet airliner, the *Comet*, developed.
- The stage musical *South Pacific* opens in New York.
- George Orwell's frightening vision of the future *Nineteen Eighty-four* published.
- The film *The Third Man* released.

# Index